For the Comfort of Automated Phrases

Jane Cassady

SiblingRivalryPress

Alexander, Arkansas
www.SiblingRivalryPress.com

For the Comfort of Automated Phrases

Copyright © 2012 by Jane Cassady.

Cover photographs by Amy Lawson. Use by permission.

Author photo by Ken Perna. Used by permission.

Cover design by Amy Lawson and Mona Z. Kraculdy.

Sibling Rivalry Press, LLC
13913 Magnolia Glen Drive
Alexander, AR 72002

info@siblingrivalrypress.com
www.siblingrivalrypress.com

ISBN: 978-1-937420-17-8

First Sibling Rivalry Press Edition, July 2012.

For Amy,
who is game for most adventures.

FOR THE COMFORT

OF AUTOMATED PHRASES

For the Comfort of Automated Phrases

For Those About to Plan Weddings, We Salute You

Married, you're responsible
for at least two sets of teeth.
Look around and count them.
You have to take care of (at least)
eight limbs, two hearts, twenty extremities
subject to frostbite.

Hone your gentle nagging
to the sound of snowfall
or the washing machine.
Budget fresh air and sunlight for you both.
Picture the week in front of you
like a staircase.

Married, you might say
Let's watch one more episode.
for the chance to lean against her heart
for another fifty minutes.
One episode may turn into seven.
It's alright.

You've doubled your books, good.
When you can lay in bed and read on Sundays
single friends might seem
a little too spur-of-the-moment.
There's someone to make you into the bed,
someone to make the coffee.

You can scrapbook a grocery-list romance

or take up birdwatching,
become almost permanently still.
The weight gain is a bother,
but the honeymoons are as many
as petals on hydrangeas.

(Unconditional love is shocking,
can make you feel invisible:
look in the mirror a lot.)

So You've Married a City,

wrote a letter to the editor and pledged it,
now you need everything at once
or to leave immediately—
it's all yours, my love, the city says,
sounding groggy as usual,
my stripped parking meters
being turned into totems,
my discussions about whether or not
it's sensitive to say
totems.

Yours, my humid field of heat
that nourishes but will not dry the laundry.
Baby, it all hangs in the air,
and when it doesn't move,
the sunsets are spectacular.

For suffering long stretches of silence,
I give you spontaneous fireworks
in poor people's yards.

Pick out names for our graffiti-faced children.
Write your plans in lake water.
They will not evaporate.

Love Poem for Tech-School Testimonials

We are educators helping you build a foundation for the future.
We are the angels of the American dream.
We are glowing with wholesome employability.
We are all mapped out in AutoCad.
We win the approval of stoic grandfathers at picnics.
There are so many picnics.
I was lost until I discovered the taupe of keyboards.
I give my testimonial in a sensible skirt,
looking out of plate-glass windows at well-ordered shrubbery.
I know spreadsheets of all species.
They wallpaper-graph the backdrops of my REM cycles.
There is ample grass where I'm living.
I wish I could get my mom to shut up about how proud she is of me.
She was afraid she would come home to a dismantled
refrigerator.
Now I fix my daughter's tricycle.
She sits on a pastel blanket.
All of her clothes are new.
I bought a motorcycle
and I drive it
to the pond.
The boys like to be in water and we like to arrange for situations
where that can happen.
My family is <u>very</u> proud of me.
I'd still be living at home.
I'd be lost if it weren't for this.
I'd be lost.

The Bi-Girl Blues

If I could change one thing,
it would be that I made my confession
while watching the World Series of Pop Culture
as you mixed rum with Coke Zero
and I wished for something to be caffeinated for.

We like romantic music.
Sometimes I want to throw my romantic music into the river
and listen to only songs that rattle the windshield,
but I come home to sappy songs just as often.

Dear men I don't really talk to anymore,
my head is clear enough to read again,
but I'm still behind on the dishes.
Dear men I still see,
thanks for being occasionally willing to hold my hand.

I can't unzip this body and crawl to the past
where my teenage self waits brazenly
at the edges of basketball courts.
To be narrower,
to cover my flaws,
hush my stupid voice.

Invocation for a Seven-Point Pew

From 10 Ways to Become an Instant Scrabble Expert:

Attitude: Keep in mind that anyone can beat anyone else with a certain amount of luck. Also remember that everyone draws poor combinations of tiles at times, so when you do, take pleasure in making the best plays you can. Finally, don't dwell on your mistakes. Everyone makes them, so go easy on yourself and just enjoy playing!

Oh, Scrabble,
we who are now playing
with an open dictionary,
thank you, for your lazy-susan apparatus
that lets us turn the board.
Thank you for the mild levees
separating the letters,
for the letter *s*, the letter *s*.

But oh, seven-point pew,
I do not trust the hands
that pulled out this spittle of vowels.
My luck is too broken
to reach into maroon cloth
and draw out letters,
or choose from a buffet
of carefully turned-over tiles.
I trust so little
that should I pull out a blank,
I will turn it over a few times
to make sure it's not another *i*.

Damn the better combinations
that will come to me in dreams
or in the shower.
Let me follow your advice, Scrabble,
find a place to spell *is* and *id* at once,
tally the points, turn the board.
I will not dump the pew out this time,
will not forfeit my turn.

For the Comfort of Automated Phrases
For my nephew, Quinn Carter

1.   On the third day, God created America,
cracked open the Catskills like a nut, and said
here is Audubon to wire up the birds,
here
are the birds.

Floodlands and firelands notwithstanding,
somehow road trips will still seem virtuous.
Let there be oversized resin roadside fauna,
and ice cream cones
on top of things,
and it was good.

2.   *The moving walkway is ending, please look down.*
Watch the tram car, please.
The autistic boy voices his concerns on the bus,
repeat.
Welcome to, route twenty
three, with service to, Broad, and Oregon.
The moving walkway is ending.
Watch the tram car please.
The rhythm of buses becomes routine,
becomes sleep.

3.   First I place you on the front step,
lift your face up to mine and ask,
"Do you want to go to the fireworks?"
You have one sneaker on.
Attempts at the other make you shriek
and cry and lay down and as I hug you,
you have the strongest elbows.
You do not want to go to the fireworks
sponsored by the nuclear power plant.
You'd rather stand
in a dark tool shed
with a spelling game.

The nuclear fireworks had lightning behind them.
When I return, smelling like Off!
and pre-nostalgia,
you are asleep on a vent.
Your face is the sweetest face
there is.

For Slim Wallace, Tour Guide at Sun Studios, Memphis, TN

Untouched by Graceland,
but amused by the variety
of Elvis-brand hot sauce,
I found a yellow postcard,
read the simple pamphlet map
and there it was,
just as the rain stopped torrenting,
guitar over the door,
Moon Pies at the counter.
You were just moving the velvet rope
and going upstairs.

You call people *cool cats*
in casual conversation.
I want to marry your *R*'s
when you tell us Jerry Lee Lewis, the Killer,
still has gigs around here
every night.

This is how distortion was invented:
the amp fell off a car-roof
and they stuffed it with newspaper.

This is how Elvis was invented:
he told a pretty secretary
he really loved his mom.

After photographs through glass

of heavy sound equipment,
after Marian's desk (Do Not Sit),
the acoustically-perfect room:
every clap is swallowed.
This is the original tile.

You direct our attention
to the photo above my head: Johnny Cash, heartthrob.
The percussion on "Walk the Line" sounds like
they might be hitting a snare with some type of brush,
but what he would do is he would fold up a dollar
at the bottom of the neck of the guitar.
Yes, this is my favorite part of the tour.
You demonstrate along with the recording:

I keep the ends out for the ties that bind...
because you're mine,
I walk the line.

They shouldn't put these guitars so near us.
We should've opened the pianos
to see how smoothed down the keys.
The microphone is available for souvenir photos,
as are you,
and posing with you, Slim Wallace,
is the happiest I've ever looked in a picture.

And though I ran back to the car
to get a book of music poems
to put in your "Don't Be Cruel" tip jar,
I heard you telling another tourist that
tonight you and your (I swear) Ol' Lady

were going to do some bowling and then
see about some motorcycles,
I know your face has never been
bathed in blue computer light;
you won't look me up.

Slim Wallace, every song should have the dollar.
For you, I would buy a million yellow
souvenir CDs, listen all down the Music Highway
where the trees are blooming purple.
I'll keep renting movies to see that room again.
Almost to Elizabethtown, I'll sob my Rilo-Kiley heart out
for near-dead relatives and redbuds
feedback and piano, and dad gummit,
I'll still keep driving.

History of the Moon Pie, Memphis, TN

There it was, sold at a lunch counter
with souvenir guitar picks:

They asked him, if he invented a snack,
what would it be like,
and drawing with his hands a circle
smaller than the original moon
larger than anything Little Debbie might coat
with industrial ganache
he said
It would be about this big.

Oh, mysterious provenance of graham,
the edible slow, my body held together
by marshmallow, grains
swelling my throat like tannins
or lust, oh sweet stars, oh
artificial banana, oh soft-spring tourist trap.
Never again in my finite life will I taste this.

As the last bugs of the Music Highway
are being squeegeed off the windshield,
I contemplate buying another,
a mini-moon,
but this one would be stale and disappointing.
It's already too far behind us.

Dear Nervous Charlie's Truckstop, Fireworks, and Souvenirs, Rt. 65, Kentucky,

Before we get to the Morning Glories,
please tell me that some of these tchotchkes,
the aproned ladies in three sizes,
the Dixie-flag shotglasses,
are only bought by installation artists of color.

We need this many fireworks, warehouses worth,
individual sparklers for some reason shaped like chickens,
baseball-themed Fireball Gift Packages, we need
Spring Showers and violet ashtrays,
beaded coin purses and state-shaped magnets.
We need to risk limbs a little,
to light gunpowder shells
and hold them burning over our heads
to simulate halos.
Oh Heavenly Splendor, oh Cover the Night,
oh spark the Strange Color of our sweet, guilty eyes.
We have stood in front of glass in Texas Cyclones.
Tomorrow we will be Moon Travelers.

The ladies in front of us take forever to fix up their coffee,
stand gabbing to the clerk, and why shouldn't they?

Dear highway, dear rest stops, we are a
Mad Dog Triple Whistle With Report,
Clustering Bees Rocket,
Sky Jamboree Night Parachute.
We can see how big it is now,
and we need to cover the sky.

I Just Want to Have Sex with Austin in General,

for the way it shifts in its seat, smirking
instead of answering the question,
the way you have to eat sugar to live,
mouth full of fruit
and humid drawl.
I have already collapsed for it,
veins racing, legs like standing in waves.
I will limp
for a week.
The city looks amused but loving
at my face as my limbs sublimate.

This is my first experience with armpit stains, be gentle.
The bell tower will remind us when
to turn our pink scalps to the cool wall,
freeze or combust,
surrender to the runaway effects of freon,
to the music of conspiracy radio.
Careful, I may swoon in the wrong direction.

Tomorrow, we will live somewhere
where we can take a walk
but until then,
my name is dissolved in salt water,
and I have never seen a cloud.

Dear Orange County 2000-2001,

Sometimes I pretend
that I can love anyone else as much
as your seascape dealing, crystal sculpting,
smiling painted-dolphin hating, sunset
pausing, water reclaiming, sprinkler timing,
lost-soul converting, Capistrano swallowing,
paint-splotch flower bordering,
Mexican-food appropriating, tide kissing,
pool backflipping, hot-tub boiling,
fake-stream landscaping, calla-lily harboring,
artichoke-thistle vilifying, armpit sweating,
seashell collecting,
Guadalupe collecting, candle vigiling,
Milagro pocketing, sunflower coaxing,
dashboard refracting, faint-star spotting,
Sunday mariachi-ing, spaghetti-strap toying,
Rubyfruit Jungling, pillow-chocolate placing,
candy-rave-snuggling wildfire face, wearing transcendent
makeup to cover fatigue, writing disguised
as a search for love, and vice versa.

I sat in Ryan's SUV and wouldn't let him go home,
said *Love is so far away.* And it never was,
wanted him to kiss me, like I always want
almost everyone to kiss me,
and later it appeared in a song
"Love is so far away, love carries us away..."
And Ryan's still touring with that song and that golden hour
4am or 4pm when I realized I had to leave you,
flattened, exhausted, borrowing money for groceries.

I was all angles then,
and when I saw you eight years later
in a bar in Philadelphia,
maybe you noticed that my face, everything had softened,
maybe you thought Los Angeles thoughts about that,
a brief flash of *US Weekly* before remembering,
We're just like us.
Adulthood suits you,
and we've learned so much since then
about bodies.

Dear Ladies of the Plano, Texas, Zumba Class,

I love you,
all one hundred and twenty of you
spaced out evenly for elbow room,
especially Cousin Marci, beauty queen,
and sister-in-law Terri, birthday girl.
We woke up early like bridesmaids.
People will ask us all day if we're sore.

You are so beautiful.
I can follow your arms but not your feet.
This body is made for booty shaking,
but not in an organized fashion.
Today is the only time
I've ever managed to clap in unison,
how did you do that?
And why did I pass up an opportunity
to wear a skirt made of coins?

This isn't dancing, it's too well lit.
I will never lose self-consciousness,
will never learn to make my hands
Bollywood-perfect like Marci does.
But smiles bubble up, unbidden.
I can stamp and rumble the floor,
count with you, sweat with you,
and oh, I will miss you,
but when I'm back in Philadelphia
dancing at the Dreamboat House
in a rally to support

taking the gender stickers off the bus passes,
you and me, ladies, thank goodness,
we'll be dancing to the same
lukewarm Christina Aguilera song from *Burlesque*.

We are a burlesque,
with nobody to see us but ourselves.
I'll never be as graceful, or as cheerful, or as fast
but when the music cuts out
I can be just as determined
to count out the steps and turns and laugh
and put my arms over my head
so that my heart will beat more with you,
my heart does beat with you, ladies, it does.

When the music cuts out for good,
and the guy comes in to tinker with the stereo
I can feel your frustration under my feet.
It's global.
It earthquakes the shiny floor.
We need this—we need to kickbox the air
and shake our asses and clap and rattle and stomp
and praise everything we've been holding back.
We need you to please fix the music.

Dear Jaimes,

You were the best thing
that ever happened to me
in the back of a van.
You drove around with a cocoon of pillows
and a stack of meticulously-catalogued
pornography.
You slept to the sound of street noise,
showered at the health club.
Mostly I hope you're indoors these days.
I hope you're still yelling at God when the car dies—
someone has to be the one to say it.
When the broken alternator started flickering the clock,
you were the vehicle.
You carry it all on your back.
You're not the only one who takes God's mistakes personally.
We threw our five-star gala tantrums in harmony.
It was so long ago.
Though mostly I try not to be broken,
light shines out the cracks anyway,
as we modulate our sorrows
and parse out our gust-voiced rages.
How are you?

Dear Shiny Little Pink Katana Phone from 2006,

Let's not fool ourselves and call this an upgrade.
Yes, I wanted a keyboard, but this new phone will never be you.
I haven't transferred all the numbers yet,
but they are an excuse for maudlin conversations:
no need to type in
Grandpa's last number
or the Upstate New York landline
marked "Home"
and illustrated with a tiny thumbnail
of a yellow living room—these
are the reasons to keep you charged.
Oh, I miss you already.

And oh, the locked texts,
though they don't always stay locked forever—
gone is "Sorry I haven't been in touch.
I've been doing nothing but getting ready for your party,
and a surprise I think you'll like."
which turned out to be a rockabilly version
of Lady Gaga's *Paparazzi*
in a wig decorated with cupcakes,
the most life-altering instance
of cross-cross dressing.

Gone also are "I was just thinking of you.
Today's drive is beautiful."
and
"How were the Mountain Goats?"
Some texts come with numbers

I can no longer call,
but these were saved:

The reminder that whenever I'm scared
of some new creative endeavor
I only need to think of Mummers.

and

"MagicPalxoxxxxoxoxoxoxo"
received just after I kissed a friend goodbye
and before I stopped
to buy flowers for my wife,
hydrangeas at 30th Street Station.

And your wallpaper, pink phone,
my wife and niece,
out for bagels and beatific.
How much luck can one little phone hold
locked or unlocked?

Dear new phone,
you really are lovely,
and you have your share
of little souvenirs, a birthday already, a farewell dinner,
a cute boy and/or dead-end crush,
the pep talks from my various one-person support groups.

But new phone,
I don't move on easily.
I don't trust your nifty menu
of symbols that allows me

to send icons of love letters
or shamrocks or cups of coffee.
Just to be sure,
I still spell my hearts
with a carrot and a three,
just to make sure everyone gets them.

The Problem with Human-as-Muse, Part One:
Contents May Have Shifted During Flight.
For Ben Trigg

She walks the liminal grey of the jetway,
pockets boarding pass, memorizes seat number.
She greets the flight attendant, thinks
Why not stewardess, but still waitress?
The Muse always has the window seat, obviously.
She clips the seat belt and adjusts to fit,
chews tough gum to relieve the pressure of takeoff,
watches the individual lights
and synapse-fires
where her friends live
turn into a blanket of amber and ozone,
pulls that over herself,
balls up a fleece under her ear
and wakes up three airports later—
Ladies and gentlemen,
we've begun our initial descent.

The Problem with Human-as-Muse, Part Two: In Line at the Post Office, The Muse Contemplates the Forever Stamp.

She waits in the little nylon maze
armload of hopeful, but not too hopeful
self-addressed, stamped envelopes
and letters to friends, barely reachable,
legible, legible now because she gave up handwriting.

She has one stamp left at the old price.
She will have to buy a stamp fragment.
She'd thought the stamp that would always work,
the one with the Liberty Bell and marked "Forever"
was an April Fool when she first heard about it.
There's something funny about the math
and how will you save it long enough?

Everyone has a drawer for "Forevers" like these.
Upon entry, they become less useful
and lose their identity,
wasted like undeveloped disposable cameras
and popsicle-making molds.

And what about adhesive?
Won't they yellow?
Won't they flake off
like that Vonnegut joke about art?
Non-archival. Not forever.

Your Art Historian Daughter Has Never Been Prouder

On the way home from the Thanksgiving weekend
when my first niece was born
and New York City was still trying to find its breath,
we stopped at the Metropolitan Museum of Art
on the way home from my sister's in-laws on Long Island.

I like to be alone in museums,
so we looked around separately,
but when we met up outside the Abstract Expressionists
he said

I was looking at this red painting that covered a whole wall
and I realized oh, I get it!
It's just red.

A History of American Wilderness in Art

But I confess that I am now
inclined to think that there is
a finer way of studying ornithology than this...

     - Thoreau, Walden

First: A graphic description
of hummingbird violence
on flowers.

Then: The artist cellophaned
with feathers and blood,
his tree trunk storm
of pointed chimney swallows,
stuffed into pockets and shirt-flaps
like penny candy.

John James Audubon *shot*
the first kingfisher (he) *saw,*
strung it to life with filed wires.
He said *it looks as if alive*
if you pull its eyelids back.

Fortune Cookie Poem #1

Love is like a sweet nectarine, good to the last drop.

She woke up, showered, left,
returned to a warm dinner,
or not.
Her drive was long.
I told her to stop texting while driving.
She got a hands-free device.
Still, talking
reduces awareness of what's around you.
As I walked home, past the funeral
flower shop, Chinese stores,
and Revolutionary War battlefield,
I forgot to tense my shoulders,
to walk with purpose.
Neither of us has died yet
from inattention.

Dear Pennsylvania,

You were the road I walked down
when I ran away from home,
the route renamed, untraceable,
but my mother's lilacs,
still stronger than anything.

Pennsylvania,
my Rumspringa,
the choice made once, stay or go.

I moved to Philadelphia
so that I could say every day
Wissahickon.

Drive north
to my family's arbitrary landmarks.
We count everything in rest stops.
We fondly remember the Electric City.
We shop carefully at Amish STUFF Etc.

I have loved your neatly-marked tunnels
through mountains
since I was born.
Hazardous materials,
please take alternate route.
Remove sunglasses.
Did you remember to turn
your headlights off?
We worry about your batteries.

Love Poem, City Blizzard

A work crush, pretty girl,
is like cabin fever,
and I need a calm, sound escape route,
should start digging.

But after the snow day I return
with pink and frozen cheeks
to walk in sidewalk footprints.
You're stuck to me like frost,
stuck in my head like a song,
as I pass each family
shoveling out one parking space each
then dragging out two chairs to claim it,
and never shabby chairs either.
The better the patio furniture,
the more claimed the space.

Home from work and trying to sleep,
my sensitive ears hear past
the ever-present baseline,
past the plow on trolley tracks
and the cats knocking things off tables—
the quiet scraping in my chest
pretty girl, tiny shovel
scraping out a rectangle,
making sure the corners are sound
enough to accommodate snow tires,
scraping the pavement bare so you don't slip,
and then, the quieter scrape
of you pulling out the furniture.

Or Just the Cost of Caring for Cats

Under the bed I found
a hibernation of fleas.
Flip the mattress, she said.
The party is almost here and so
we cleaned with our whole bodies,
the yoga of wintertime—
I knew the moldy windowsills,
the advanced spiders, but this—
Flip the mattress, she said—
they were flat on their brown sides
not a flurry or even a lot,
just a tiny autumn of fleas,
a sprinkling—my life as a vacuum
cleaner commenced, sucking brick dust
and fragments of lost Saturdays in bed.
One crawled though your hair
like a lazy Surrealist
while you smiled at me from your pillow.
One hopped across my *Entertainment Weekly*.
The vacuum bags are on the porch to freeze them,
but they can lie dormant for years.
Is this the thing that's been hunting us forever,
our debt taken in small nicks and irritation,
a bouquet of apologies
in a circle of bites?

Hostile Work Environment

I wish you no worse than your own commute,
garments against the drizzle
shielding your own safe face,
while mine is a membrane of jokes, a ghost.

Your garments against the drizzle,
I am an X-ray peep show, a fish bowl.
I remain a membrane of jokes, a ghost,
in the comfort of paranoia confirmed.

I am an X-ray peep show, a fish bowl.
I'm not crazy, you're just awful,
my comfort in paranoia confirmed,
cells no longer shocked to move.

I'm not crazy, you're just awful,
and of course I was being watched, throat cut,
bones no longer coaxed to move,
but panic, a visceral clock.

Of course I was being watched, throat cut.
Bone-scraped daily, I did not develop thick skin,
just panic, a visceral clock,
you hear me, just barely, scraped and skinless.

Scraped daily, I did not develop thick skin,
but a festering chorus, a bloody cacophony.
You hear me, just barely, scraped and skinless,
blush-mortified, paralyzed with doubt.

You festering chorus, you bloody cacophony,
learn to control your facial expressions,
blush-mortified, paralyze yourself with doubt.
I wish you the crush of sadness you rolled your eyes at.

I've learned to control my facial expressions,
shield my own safe face.
I wish you the crush of sadness you rolled your eyes at.
I wish you no worse than your own commute.

Fortune Cookie Poem #2
Soon, your old friends will remind you of your forgotten childhood joys.

It was all fresh air
and helplessness that summer.
Sleep was like falling down a hole,
lunch was a lifeboat.
This was before I started living
on crudites and ice cream.
When I could sit on the back of a tied pony
and read a book.
The first alarm clock:
a sunrise like lilac water,
slightly singed toast,
grapefruit spoons.
It was my idea to make the special breakfast.
Naming the rocks was, too.

Against the Dissolution of Old-Timey Words for Kissing

Makeout Session:
she, with her waistbanded obsolete figure
drops the scarf, the race can begin.
There's danger of skidding,
the temptation to hydroplane.

Heavy Petting:
Here, sure hand under pearls, pearls everywhere,
the backs of your eyelids iridescent,
sand's time spent with a wayward mollusk.

A Smooch:
A little more adult.
They test the progression of sun-angles
on grass after rain.

Or soapsuds wiped off on an apron.
Love walks into soup-vapor,
smelling like flannel and snow.

Making Soup for a Work Friend while *Lost* Is On

Five nights ago, reaching like kids do,
your daughter stood up in her shopping cart seat,
reached a little too much, and slipped.
She fell
like a jar.
The boundaries of her skull and brain
lost their fidelity.

Now,
the surgery successful,
you worry over her cute hair
interrupted by a scar.

Now you can't not go back to the grocery store,
and boiling water is my affectation,
so that I would know what to do
when there's nothing to be done.
When my mom was crashed into
by an ambulance
and called me about pools of blood
on the car roof,
when my wife's shin opened
like tissue paper
and made me hate the word suture
forever.

And tonight, while Lily comes home to her own bed,
your family relearns how to sleep,
and you watch that show we talk about at work
I cut up carrots and meat into small cubes.

It is absolutely stupid of me
to write about something so much yours,
but we are halved
by the same blade,
all of us, soup and blood.

On the Way Home from the *Twin Peaks* Art Show

Having gotten there too late to judge the pie contest,
finding only ugly, decimated crusts,
I braved after a few minutes
pulling aside the red drapes
finding the floor to be zigzagged rather than checkerboard
the way I remembered it.
In a collage/painting, her green-lit body
strobed and crawling through the woods,
her world of tar pits and flashlight circles.
The terror she must've felt as she crawled,
as she was bound and pecked at.
I was thinking as we drove past
the rowhouses of Lehigh Avenue
about surrealism's female body count,
how much pain Laura Palmer had been through
so that we could watch, eating spaghetti
on tray tables as if nothing had happened.
I rode in the car
empathizing with Laura Palmer for 17 blocks
before I remembered she wasn't real,
she never went through anything.

What the Lady in the Radiator Dreams About
When She Finally Sleeps After All These Years

Radio noise in your voice.
Aliens on the attic stairs.
Songs about snooze alarms.
Some time to look at your face.
Blouses, shoes, soft socks.
Nice ladies for the tea party.
Your voice, folded and put away
like a sheet.
Line of headlights down the canyon.
Couldn't move or startle.
Harping on exercise.
Money for carbohydrates.
Time to look at the glittery shards.
Trust-fish in the freezer.
The noise in your face.
Trouble in the body.
The narrow sound of cars.
Your trail of night lights.

An Embarrassment Of...

For Jenny Lewis and The Watson Twins' album Rabbit Fur Coat

Window seats of the world, unite.
An afternoon of gin
and intravenous chocolate cake.
It gets you in the soul
and in the underpants.
It isn't spring,
but water's moving under snow.

In Praise of Friend-Crushes

From cutting and pasting the words to Lady Gaga's "Paparazzi"

In this dance, I'm running toward you.
We don't mind the famous velvet flashing.
We don't chase safe pictures.
Ready for the biggest room in our hotel-hearts,
we look past glamorous backstage promises.
You're like the radio, if it were unpredictable.
Chase your girl.
Follow the light until you keel over,
until you love me.
Sure as photo-flashes,
you're the glitter in my eyelashes.
I know the crowd's here,
but I can't hear them.
You're my price coming down,
and I'll need that, I'll know your famous face.
We don't have to wait at appropriate distances.
I'll be burnt sparklers,
plastic rings from gumball machines, 4-EVER.
(For eva eva? For eva eva.)

Between the true slumber party dance
and the studio sets,
I'll follow you.

Beyoncé is Better at Having Feelings than I Am
From cutting and pasting the lyrics to "Halo"

Everything I pray for
is a little bit embarrassing.
Your halo is really the least of it.
Awake, saving it up like the sun,
every risk that gravity won't forget,
that I won't even remember the ground.
I accidentally built burning,
can't fade grace again.
I feel like tumbling, halo.
I feel surrounded.
I swore I'd never write this,
now it's written.
Like a standing ray on addicted walls,
I can't embrace you out, angel.
Haven't found a fight again.
I had more doubt over this.
You're looking,
maybe.
It's the falling.

Letter from the Divine Whatever to the Newly Out

From cutting and pasting the words to Lady Gaga's "Born This Way"

Darling,

I'm on the way.
You were born ready to orient yourself,
and no other way.

Track decades like starfields.

I love this record and I love you.

Be ready to transubstantiate.

Go far, outcast or enveloped, usually both.

Who you are is a religion.

When I was stars,
I didn't have to put lipstick on
or look in the mirror, now I'm everything.

We're all born supersensitive to the light.
It's rolled across space like blankets.

No one mistakes
beautiful for regret,
descent for prudence,
teased for broke.

Ooo, there's you, a fresh meteor,

streaking straight across the insecure sky.

Rejoice, kid,
the universe is young.

Love,
Your Friends

Contents of a Chick-Lit Heroine's Yard Sale

Clothes that used to fit.
Rainbow tube top, belonging to carefree younger sister.
High school year book, his.
Lingerie, LaPerla, purple, still in gift box.
Snowglobe from the tree lighting.
Ice skates.
Cell phone bedazzling kit, slightly used.
Underwear, days of the week, missing Wednesday.
Cookbook, "Hello Cupcake."
Baby blanket, yellow.
Bridesmaid dresses, implausible.
So many pillar candles.
The Best of Depeche Mode, Volume 1.
Audrey Hepburn Ultimate Collection DVDs.
Engagement ring in Tiffany box.
Lucite heels with cherries on the toes.
Portfolio, battered.
Bachelorette veil and sash.
Handbag, as is. (broken strap)
Stilettos, as is. (broken heel)
Secret Camel pack w/blue Bic lighter in the cellophane.
Writing desk.
Florist vases, two dozen.
Various silver-wrapped gifts, unopened.

Philadelphia Mix Tape

Or: Why It Was My 2009 New Year's Resolution To Be More Like Beyoncé.

1.   For the price of taking a tract,
        a choir on the sidewalk.

2.   When the soon-to-be President spoke in the park, he
        was unprepared for call-and-response.

3.   In line at Pathmark, a woman crooning
        "If I were a boy..." over her shopping cart.

4.   Waiting for a bus, South Philly, March: the bricks
        reverberate with rehearsing Mummers.

5.   Unitarian cantata on the life of Harriet Tubman.

6.   A political argument boils down as someone says,
        "Boy, they play a lot of Pixies in here."

7.   The cars, the buildings, the school hallways,
        even the mockingbirds go
        "wee oo wee oo weet, wee oo wee oo weet..."

8.   On a date, my wife and I pay a dollar a second
        to a busker whose steel guitar wafts us up the stairs
        and out from the Regional Rail.

9.   The club behind our house (and I do mean RIGHT
        behind our house) makes our 3am bones ache to
        comply with the instructions of R&B line dances.

10. My first memory (age 2): families lay on the floor
    in the middle of Wanamaker's (now Macy's) watching
    the Christmas light show accompanied by a store-sized
    pipe organ that rivals the one in Arcade Fire's
    "Intervention."

11. Speeches from shop-front speakers:
    our most remixed President.

12. A bus full of kids on the way to the skating rink
    sprouts, then blooms, then becomes a full blown
    "All the Single Ladies" sing along, complete with moves.
    (Fadeout in whoh-oh-ohs...)

Song for the Job-Quitters

There is more love somewhere.
There is more love somewhere.
I'm gonna keep on
'til I find it.
There is more love somewhere.

> *- Hymn*

When you go to collect your belongings
may you not leave a pencil case behind.
May a shaft of sun shine through the industrial windows
in a show of solidarity.
May your boss be out of the office.
When someone asks if you don't work there anymore
may you be unable to wipe the smile off your face.

May you mourn the lost phone numbers,
blanket stillborn projects
and float them out on paper boats.

May you walk those blocks again when you're ready
see the azaleas in all their madness.

May you take cryptic advice from church signs,
list "The Universe" as a source of income
and mean it.

May the duvet whisper sweet nothings.
If you can't get out of bed,
may a cat sit on you.

May you lose the days of the week.

May you leave yourself a maze of flares
across the bridges.

May you walk into kinder rooms
to the dazzling realization:
maybe it wasn't just you.

Gifts for Seven Fools, Including Me

To the podcast host
who made me cry on Twitter
when he called me *shrill and overly corrective*,
based on a grand total of two tweets:
first I give you my tears, of course,
because modern times are unmanageable
and I've learned that if I'm gonna
fill my ears with strangers,
they'd better have guitars.

Next I give you the first crack
of some new metaphorical whip,
my subscription to *Bitch Magazine*,
and every political argument
I've ever had via Facebook comments.
They're all yours, a blue-gray bouquet.

To the poor guy who used to cut my mats
in Photography school,
who briefly called me "Mistress":

1.   Thank you for drawing me as Tank Girl.

2.   I'm sorry that I cut up your comic books to make
        collages. I'm sure I'm still paying the karmic debt.

So I give you all of the naïve/slutty self-portraits
I took for mediocre grades.
(I'll mat and frame them myself, I promise.)

And I give you also someone nicer
(but not too much nicer)
to go see *The Crow* with,
and fresh strawberries from street vendors
to eat on the way home.

To the ex-girlfriend
who found me on MySpace
and then wrote a many-paragraph post
about how she'd had a nightmare about me
wherein I said she couldn't love anybody else
eight years after the fact:

Oh, Erin Ballantine, I give you
my entire poetry career.

From that day, way before social networks,
when we broke up for real
and I sat outside Human Evolution Class
at the Laguna Beach College of Art and Design
crying my face off
and to cheer me up,
my friend Kilby said
Let's go see some poetry,
and I said *sure*, and after that,
I wrote poems,
so here, everything I've written since.

To my first Muse/the last man I slept with,
I give you (DAMMIT!)
a couple more stanzas:
I give you Laguna Canyon in a fog-lost freeway,

sticky waves on my feet like a movie
lady bug pajamas for good luck,
theatrical groans that woke the grizzled landlord,
a startled dragonfly,
a Glass Menagerie for your blue rose tattoo.

I give you back this response
to handing you my first love poem:

Is that where you're gonna put your line breaks?

I give you breakfast, Memorial Day, 2000.
I give you the continued allegiance
of mix tapes,
and the promise, if I could go back, I'd believe you
when you said it was just that night.

To the woman who almost ran me over
after I sent her a love poem:
I give you every love poem since,
not the content, just the stupid bravery,
the cold adrenaline of risk
knowing I might lose everything,
but still pressing "Send."

To the contempt-faced boss
who decided children weren't safe around me
after I got a crush on a coworker:
I have nothing for you but glitter,
great queer mountains and drifts of it.
I've revisited my last day
and shaken out every size, shape and color,

and sequins for every holiday
over every desk and chair,
over the arts and crafts supplies
stacked in orange milk crates,
over your unfinished paperwork,
over the pictures of family
that you were allowed to hang up and I wasn't.
Good luck cleaning it up.

Dear Philadelphia,

I'm embarrassed that it took me
so long to love you, or
once the winter came
progress was halted,
I could leave on my coat
and stand by the door,
in case I was asked to leave.

I've never been sure
a place was made for me anywhere,
like I hadn't been put on some list,
and ever since I left California
on a midnight bus to two trains
I'm afraid to have friends in the same city,
lest I should have to pare down my belongings,
buy souvenir diner T-shirts,
and echo along on my own again.

But you know what, I surrender,
your openhearted narrow streets,
trolley-tracked arterials from one room
of lightning-crack hearts to the next.
The skyline that coordinates its lights
according to the occasion—
what color for cracked chest
like a museum of butterflies?

I can no longer keep you at arm's length,
wavy glass of the Continental Congress,

pennies on Ben Franklin's grave;
being a tourist with your own apartment nearby
is like a second honeymoon,
the startled relief of *I found you and I get to stay.*

A friend says *I didn't like it last time.*
I couldn't see where they get their beauty.
Like it's a nutrient, and it is.
Today, white petals floated down
from one particularly generous tree,
onto an audience agreeing to the same
blood, the same air.

Philadelphia, I will learn not to feel threatened.
Let me make it up to you,
I will save every ticket stub,
fortune and petal.

Love Poem with Traditional Anniversary Gifts

Shred the bills and soak the paper,
cotton together a place on the couch.

Never mind the leather hearts that voted against us,
I'm building you a house out of flowers and fruit.
(Stronger than wood, to postpone the burning.)

Festoon it with garlands of candy,
iron the perfect sheets.

I'm melting all of your heads-up pennies,
to make us copper cups.

I've had Saturday mornings bronzed for us,
buried the broken pottery.
(You can willow it out if you want.)

Never mind the aluminum music
of the Tuesday night recycle bin,
and maybe, darling, bad luck isn't made of steel.

I'm embroidering silk pillows
with all your equations,
linen tablecloths of elements—
what falls through the lace, leave it.
Don't worry the edges.

Roll the ivory dice and smash the crystal.
Our china is patterned in contemporary verse

and TV plots.

What's in your shoulder bag, flashing silver?

What do pearls do besides annoy oysters?

Do mistakes grow their own coral?

Do we have enough ruby in our blood?

Can we go to Cape May
and look at the ocean till it turns to sapphires?

Do you believe in gold?

When will you weedwack
the emerald backyard?

Will you plant me some facets, diamond?

Some Made-Up Memories Because I Miss You

We met in the Duchamp Room
at the Philadelphia Museum of Art,
The Rrose Sélavy Gallery.
You looked in at *Étant Donnés*
and were surprised, but not that surprised
by what you saw.
We agreed that the little moving waterfall was the best part.

Then we committed our own
unspeakable acts of Dadaism
in the third-floor stairwell
with the big view of the skyline
while I patiently parsed out the iconography
of *The Bride Stripped Bare By Her Bachelors, Even*
commonly referred to
as *The Large Glass.*

We met at my first rock concert,
though I have no idea what the heck you were doing
at an Aerosmith/Skid Row show,
they are totally not metal enough for you.
I was there with my mom.
You explained why there was so much swearing
and you charmed her,
which might be why I didn't call.

Still, you were the one who taught me
that you never wear a band's T-shirt
to that band's show.
You were the one who taught me how to smoke.
You were the tingle in my jaw,

the shortness of breath.
By the time I was busy losing my virginity
to a Cinderella song,
I knew you would've chosen a better track.

We met at a writing conference
on neutral ground,
some anonymous mountain
overlooking a paradigmatic lake.

The cabin walls were soundproof,
like the other room in sitcoms
but I yelped and shrieked
and shattered the panes from the windows.
You were so cute, picking the shards from my hair.
When the proprietors came to sweep up the glass,
they brought Jameson and breakfast.
We never had to leave.
We never had to remember
what Shakespeare said about the goddamn birds.

Surprisingly, we got a lot of writing done.
I still blush when I hear the word *sonnet*.

We met while the house was still burning down.
You had a sublet.
You spent every evening
snuffing the standby lights of appliances
so I wouldn't mistake them for flames.
You washed the smell of smoke out of everything.
You were so *careful*.

To Amy and the Rained-Out Science Carnival

I'm sorry
I can't imagine what we would've seen,
what beakers of fireworks
what Bunsen burner tilt-a-whirl
what Mobius Ferris wheel
what Fibonacci weight-guess
what golden mean funhouse
what periodic-table bingo
what bent-space ring toss
what juggling heartbeats
what X-ray hand-puppets
what cotton candy cumulus
what orbiting petting zoo
what luck-prisms and tear-agates
what birds of rare minerals,
because what gravity, what heat, what light to my relief
that I can crawl back into bed with you
with nothing but library books.

Acknowledgements, Notes, & Previouslies

"For the Comfort of Automated Phrases" is owed to a writing prompt from Roger Bonair-Agard. "First I place you" comes from the poem "Now I'm Building the World" by Vincent Cioffi.

"So You've Married a City" is for Syracuse, NY.

The Antenna (Poetry and Art Journal of Scranton, PA): "Love Poem for Tech-school Testimonials."

Apiary: "Song for the Job Quitters" and "Dear Pennsylvania."

Ballard Street Poetry Journal: "Invocation for a Seven-Point Pew."

Certain Circuits: "Against the Dissolution of Old-Timey Words for Kissing."

Danse Macabre: "Or Just the Cost of Caring for Cats."

decomP: "Fortune Cookie Poem #2."

Imagination & Place: "So You've Married a City."

Lavender Review: "Love Poem With Traditional Anniversary Gifts."

The Legendary: "Love Poem, City Blizzard," "In Praise of Friend-Crushes," "On the Way Home from the Twin Peaks Art Show," "What the Lady in the Radiator Dreams About When She Finally Sleeps After All These Years," "For Slim Wallace, Tour Guide at Sun Studios, Memphis, TN," "History of the Moon Pie, Memphis, TN," "Dear Orange County 2000-2001," and "Dear Philadelphia."

The November Third Club: "Dear Nervous Charlie's Truckstop, Fireworks, and Souvenirs, Rt. 65, Kentucky," and "For the Comfort of Automated Phrases."

Poetry Superhighway: "An Embarrassment Of..."

Radius: "In Praise of Friend Crushes" (as an invented form) and "Letter from the Divine Whatever to the Newly Out."

Used Furniture Review: "A History of American Wilderness in Art."

Special thanks to Inevitable Press (Pat and Marcia Cohee), Hard Times Press (Daniel McGinn), and Turtle Ink Press (my sweet wife, Amy Lawson), in whose chapbooks some of these poems have appeared.

About the Poet

Jane Cassady probably wants to hug you. She writes "Poetic License Horoscopes" for Sibling Rivalry Press, *The Legendary*, and *Critical Mass*, the Philadelphia City Paper's arts and culture blog. Her poems "In 1992," "Almost Immediately," "It Got Better" and "For the Comfort of Automated Phrases" can be heard on *Indiefeed: Performance Poetry*. She has been featured in *decomP, The Ballard Street Poetry Journal, Lavender Review*, and other journals. She has performed at such venues as LouderArts in New York City, Valley Contemporary Poets in Los Angeles, and The Encyclopedia Show in Chicago. She also writes a blog about happiness, love, and pop-culture called *The Serotonin Factory*.

theserotoninfactory.blogspot.com

About the Publisher

The mission of Sibling Rivalry Press is to develop, publish, and promote outlaw artistic talent—those projects which inspire people to read, challenge, and ponder the complexities of life in dark rooms, under blankets by cell-phone illumination, in the backseats of cars, and on spring-day park benches next to people reading Mindy Kaling and Miranda July. We welcome manuscripts which push boundaries, sing sweetly, or inspire us to perform karaoke in drag. Not much makes us flinch.

www.siblingrivalrypress.com

CPSIA information can be obtained at www.ICGtesting.com
Printed in the USA
LVOW081914220512

282783LV00003B/5/P